IMAGES OF ENGLAND

FILEY

FILEY
FOR THE FAMILY

Chas Pears

Illustrated booklet free from Council Offices
Filey Yorks or any L·N·E·R Enquiry Office

IMAGES OF ENGLAND

FILEY

PETER HARRIS

TEMPUS

Frontispiece: An Filey poster from between the wars.

First published 2006

Tempus Publishing Limited
The Mill, Brimscombe Port,
Stroud, Gloucestershire, GL5 2QG
www.tempus-publishing.com

British Library Cataloguing in Publication Data.
A catalogue record for this book is available from the British Library.

ISBN 0 7524 3847 6

Typesetting and origination by Tempus Publishing Limited.
Printed in Great Britain.

Contents

Foreword

The key to understanding Filey is to appreciate that, until the middle of the twentieth century, it could be seen in many ways as two separate communities. Old Filey was the original small fishing village whose population varied little over several centuries and whose residents lived in or close to what is now Queen Street. Fishing was, of course, the main occupation but, from medieval times until the late eighteenth century, many also worked on the land in the three surrounding fields; Church Field, Great Field and Little Field. For such a small community, the Parish Church of St Oswald is surprisingly large. Inclosure, which took place in 1791, saw the three fields converted into many smaller pieces of land under private ownership.

New Filey came into being as the result of the vision of an elderly Birmingham solicitor, John Wilkes Unett, who came to Filey in the early 1830s, perhaps while staying in Scarborough, and recognised the potential for careful and appropriate development of the land to the south of the village. Very fortunately, his main concern was that the new town should be worthy of its location and generations of residents and visitors have been grateful that he was successful in his venture. In fact, some would say that the combination of the imposing terrace know as The Crescent, the spacious and colourful gardens and the seaward views encompassing the Brigg, the Bay and Flamborough Head constitutes one of the finest locations in the whole of Britain.

New Filey grew quickly during the Victorian era but for many years the two communities retained their separate identities and the distinctive terms, Old and New, were included in postal addresses. Today, Queen Street has no shops but a century ago up to thirty could be found there catering to all the needs of Old Filey's residents.

From mid-Victorian days the Crescent (later Royal Crescent) Hotel and several small hotels and boarding-houses acquired, quite quickly, enviable reputations amongst discerning visitors and Filey became thought of as an attractive and select resort, popular not only with holidaymakers from West and South Yorkshire but also from the Midlands, London and the Home Counties. This conclusion is confirmed by a reference to many editions of the weekly newspaper, *The Filey Post* and List of Visitors, in which the names and home towns appear of almost everyone staying in the town.

Filey in the twenty-first century still retains its excellent reputation as a traditional seaside resort but inshore fishing as a way of life is much diminished. The building of new housing estates from the 1960s onward continues to attract new residents, many of whom see Filey as an attractive town to which to retire.

From a local historical point of view Filey has been very fortunate in the number of photographers and artists who practised their art here; in particular, of course, Walter Fisher who made his home in the town.

Peter Harris has, over many years, assembled a remarkably comprehensive collection of images of Filey and we are indebted to him for linking so many together in a way which retains our close interest as we follow Filey's story from its days as an important fishing station to its development as a very popular holiday resort.

Michael Fearon (Honourary Curator of Filey Museum)
Filey, 2006

Acknowledgements

The primary source for the photographs in this book is the author's own collection – consisting mainly of postcards – which has been built up over the last thirty years. Other images have been chosen from the Crimlisk-Fisher archives of Filey Town Council, by the kind permission of Eric Pinder, the archivist. Images have also been taken from material which is in the collection of Filey Museum, by kind permission of the trustees and Michael Fearon, who also supplied further details.

I am grateful to John Kennedy of John Hinde Ltd, publishers of Dublin, for permission to reproduce a number of pictures of Butlin's in Filey. Thanks are also due to Mrs Joanne Cammish, Mrs Elizabeth Clegg, Malcolm Johnson and Keith Tyler, who kindly allowed me to use some of their own collections and supplied valuable information. Memories and other data supplied by David Crimlisk and staff at the Filey Lifeboat Station and public library, together with many other enthusiastic Filonians, are much appreciated.

Finally, my sincere thanks must go to Miss Lisa Selby for some of the IT work, and to my wife Terry Harris for her patience, forbearance and assistance with the text.

Bibliography

Blair, Lyle, ed., *The Butlin's Holiday Book 1949-50* (Adprint Ltd).

Clegg, K., *Filey, a Select Resort*.

Ibid., transcriber, *Diary of a Schoolboy on Holiday in Filey, 1908* (1998).

Cooper, A.N. and Martin, E., *Filey Sea Wall*, facsimile edition (K. Clegg, 2000).

Fearon, Michael, *Filey: From Fishing Village to Edwardian Resort* (Hutton Press Ltd, 1990).

Ibid., *Old Filey Remembered* (Hutton Press Ltd, 1994).

Filey and the Yorkshire Coast – Red Guide (Ward, Lock & Co.).

Gower, Ted, *Filey* (Dales Publishing Co., 1977).

Kelly's Directories (1909, 1927).

Wray, Paul, *Butlin's Filey: Thanks for the Memories* (Hutton Press, 1992).

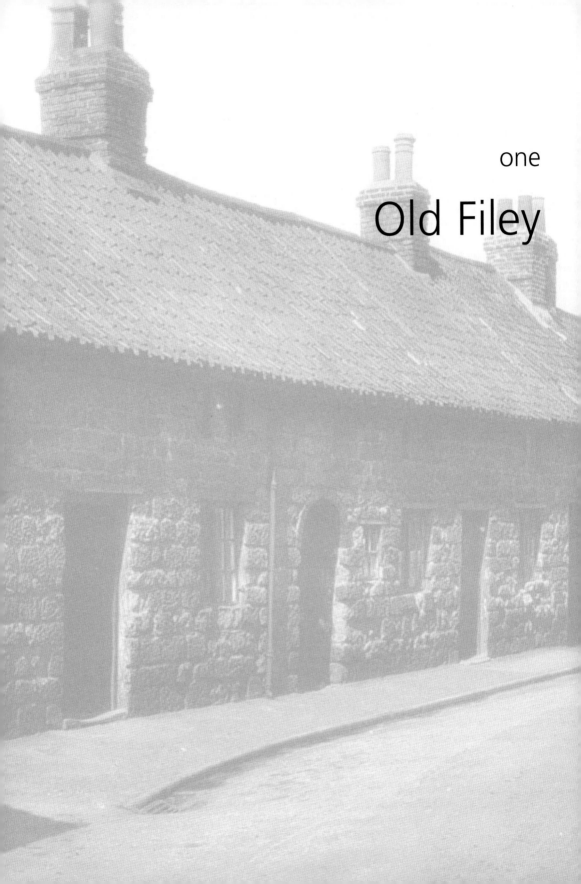

one

Old Filey

An aero-photo card, looking north, shows the extent of Filey in the early 1950s. To the distant right is St Oswald's church seen nestling within the trees of the Ravine and the concentration of cottages of Old Filey. In the foreground the impressive Crescent is clear, with the more sprawling development of the nineteenth and twentieth centuries behind.

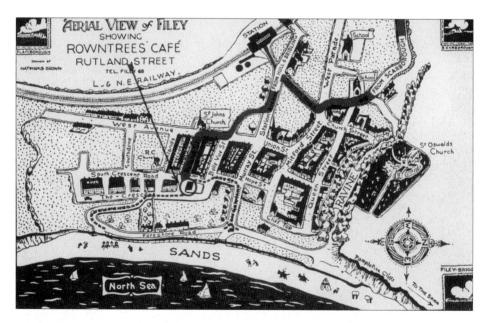

Rowntrees' Café in Rutland Street produced this helpful advertising card. It was one of the very few places at the time where it was possible to eat out. Besides showing the location of the café this card usefully maps other important thoroughfares for visitors to the town. The café has long since been replaced by apartments.

Queen Street, along with Church Street, was the nucleus of Old Filey. The many domestic building styles illustrate the gradual historical development of this intimate community. The groups of men and women here were, no doubt, discussing important issues of the day.

These stone-built cottages in Queen Street, opposite the present museum, housed a number of fishing families. Like many other building in this area they were regrettably demolished in the early 1960s and replaced with modern housing.

Left: T'Oard Ship in Queen Street was one of a number of local inns which originally served the recreational needs of this fishing community as well as the early tourists. It was reputedly the haunt of smugglers, having the usual secret cupboards and sliding panels for concealing contraband. The sign has long gone and it is now a private residence.

Below: Behind the inn was one of the dozen or so yards or 'rents' which lay behind the street frontages of the old town. Each contained their own close-knit group of families. Besides the lavatory ('t'backway') this area would be where fishing nets and gear would await repair and where other useful items might be stored. The yards might undergo a spring clean for special occasions.

Foord's Hotel, also in Queen Street, midway down the left-hand side, was built in the mid-1820s. It was a coaching house on the Scarborough to Hull route. In later years the hotel would send a coach to meet the trains at Filey Station to transfer visitors to the hotel.

GEORGE S. CAMMISH,

GROCER AND

PROVISION DEALER,

16, QUEEN STREET, FILEY.

Nothing but the Best Brand of Goods Stocked,

And always at the Lowest Possible Price.

A TRIAL ORDER INVITED.

Trade card for George S. Cammish, grocer and provision dealer of No. 16 Queen Street.

Most of these houses, belonging to fishermen, and other business premises along Queen Street had been demolished by the 1960s. Behind the wall on the left was the vicarage garden. The white building, just behind and to the right of the group of children, was saved and converted into what is now the Filey Museum.

The Filey Museum was opened in 1971 as a result of the combined efforts of the Lion's Club, the museum trustees and the town council. It was once a single-storey farmhouse dating back to 1696 and known as Gibson's Farm. In more recent times it was a dairy. The plaque over the door reads 'The Fear of God be in You'.

The buildings at Cliff Top were at the seaward end of Queen Street, here seen from the Coble Landing. Note the squared extension to one of the buildings which was the coastguard station. Fishermen and their wives would have had to carry their equipment up and down Sand Hill where the steps are.

A closer view of Cliff Top showing the coastguard station. A sign on the railings reads 'Apartments', inviting visitors to stay.

Trade advertisement of Sowden's, who were stationers in Reynolds Street, Old Filey. They also offered a circulating library and, perhaps strangely, were agents for pianos, tea and baking powder.

Above: The Smuggler's Cottage was situated in an area between Queen Street and Mitford Street, behind the Foord Hotel, in a position which overlooked the sea. The cottage contained a number of interesting features and displays of artefacts. It was occasionally opened to the public as a sort of museum in the early 1900s.

Opposite: Cammish's Boot Shop at No. 15 Reynolds Street. Seasickness and ill health prevented Robert Cammish joining the family's yawl, *Diligence*. However, after serving his apprenticeship he set up in business making fishermens' sea boots to order, a highly skilled craft. Edmund, his son, then took over the business helped by his sister Betsy.

A close-up view showing one of the secret hiding places in Smuggler's Cottage in which contraband was reputedly concealed. This was in the wall behind the front door under the rail of coat pegs and was known as the 'Smuggle Hole'.

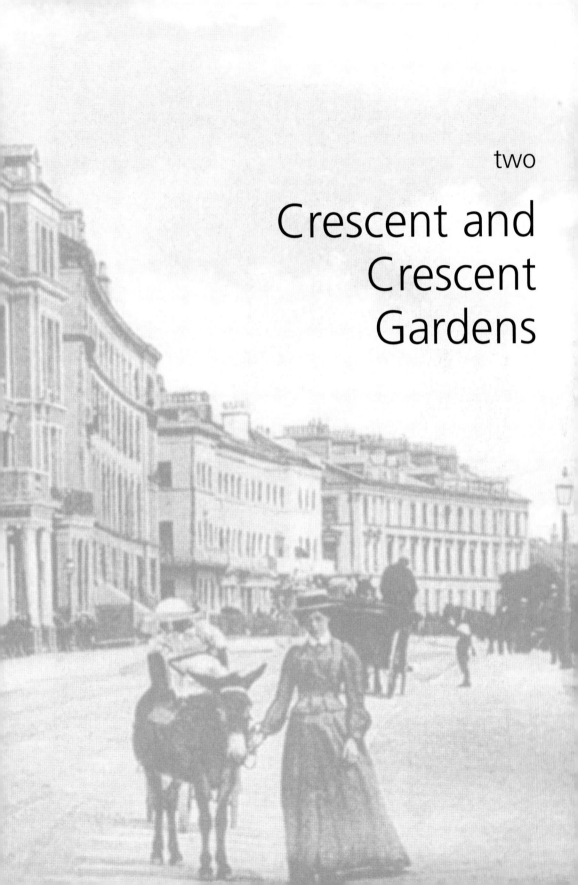

two

Crescent and Crescent Gardens

The Crescent resulted from a plan for a New Filey conceived in the 1830s by John Wilkes Unett, a solicitor from Birmingham. He eventually owned most of the land bounded by West Avenue, Murray Street, the seafront and Glen Gardens. The plots which formed the Crescent were sold to individual builders.

The first block to be built (marked with a cross) and the second one away from Murray Street, were erected at the beginning of the 1840s. The entrances were of classical Greek design and an ornate iron balcony ran along the front at first-floor level. The second block (nearest to the camera) was built by a Leeds bookshop owner in 1851.

The Royal Crescent Hotel, opened in 1853, offered a very high standard of accommodation. As was the fashion, visitors were listed each week in the *Filey Post*. They included royalty, the nobility, military officers and other VIPs who travelled there from all over Britain and the Continent, together with their attendant household staff.

This rare photograph, *c.* 1880, shows that the most southerly block had yet to be constructed. Each set of buildings was slightly different in design but all formed a pleasant and impressive range and afforded both visitors and residents fine, sweeping views of the bay.

Osborne House, at the junction of the Crescent and South Crescent, was the final building which completed the terrace and was finished in 1890 by Edwin Martin, who had recently moved into the nearby Ravine Villa.

The Crescent was kept meticulously clean, very necessary considering the equine traffic of the times.

Motor traffic began to increase significantly in the 1930s. Many of the private residences in the Crescent would have been converted into small hotels, such as the Brigg and the Victoria, or residential apartments and rented accommodation.

Crescent Garage in South Crescent Road. Smart's responded early to the dawn of the motoring age by providing garaging for the cars of visitors to the Crescent, as well as taxis, car hire, servicing and repairs. Here a 12hp Rolls Royce, registered in Leeds in 1905, is proudly pictured with Harry Smart in front of his premises.

The third development along the Crescent consisted of six boarding houses which later became the Victoria Hotel (to the left) and Ebor Court. In the 1970s the Victoria was converted back into private residences.

Part of Unett's design for New Filey included these pleasure grounds which were for the exclusive benefit of the owners and occupiers of the adjacent Crescent. It is worth noting the kerb-side stone blocks which allowed passengers a more convenient access to their carriages.

The Crescent Gardens were administered for many years by a committee who, at first, used monies raised by weekly subscriptions from the owners and occupiers of the houses along the Crescent. The committee was responsible for the planting, upkeep and policing of the enclosed area. Note the kiosk which was set up in later years to sell admission tickets to the general public.

During the summer season the committee hired a small orchestra to entertain subscribers to the garden. They performed twice a day in the open until a music stand was built in the early 1870s. This orchestra of musicians and singers was hired for the 1908 season.

FILEY. CRESCENT GARDENS.

In the 1920s a covered colonnade was built and the bandstand, around which dancing could take place, was relocated to the lower level. This in turn was remodelled in 1960 when the 'Sun Lounge' was built to replace the bandstand.

This Edwardian image of 1906 shows a typical Sunday scene when many of the public would parade over the Crescent lawns and gardens attired in their Sunday best, having attended church or finished their Sunday lunch.

In 1920 the gardens were purchased by the Filey Urban District Council and became freely open for use and enjoyment by the general public. Here visitors are relaxing and chatting.

A general view of the Crescent and foreshore. Mama is taking in the sea air while the children patiently amuse themselves.

Just to the south of the land which became occupied by the Crescent, Henry Bentley had the Ravine Hall built in 1838 and surrounded it with delightful gardens. The house was later acquired by Edwin Martin in 1889.

Filey Council purchased the hall and its grounds in 1930 and attempted to convert the building into an entertainment centre. The grounds were renamed Glen Gardens. To provide for the public, paths were laid out, flowerbeds planted, seating and shelters installed, and a putting green and boating lake opened.

Crescent Hill was the main route from the Crescent down to the beach, promenade and foreshore. Again, this was planned by John Wilkes Unett.

As a child, the ascent up Crescent Hill seemed long and steep after a day on the sands and a donkey ride up was most welcome. Chariots would also be available for the more weary.

Filey snow scenes are scarce, possibly because such images may not have conveyed the desirable holiday image of the resort. Here, the normally cobbled surface of Crescent Hill has been temporally covered by the recent fall.

three

New Filey

Belle Vue Street looking seaward, c. 1904. Henry Walker's greengrocery occupies the corner shop, while Simpson's and the library are further down on the right. The Old Royal Hotel, on the left, never proved viable and was demolished in the mid-1930s.

A 1920s view of Belle Vue Street looking inland, showing the Belle Vue private hotel, the chemist and other shops.

Right: Semadeni & Sons, a bread and confectionery shop seen here in 1906, offered a range of tempting cakes, biscuits, sweets and more. The proprietor was the first Italian to run a business in Filey. The shop was in Murray Street, below the Three Tuns and where Sterchi's the confectioner now trades.

Below: Trade advertisement for Crawford's, general draper and outfitter on the corner of Belle Vue Street and John Street, which is now a charity shop.

ROBERT CRAWFORD,

Linen Draper, Silk Mercer, Gent.'s Outfitter,

Mantles, Underclothing, Family Mourning,

CARPETS, BEDSTEADS, FURNISHINGS,

Corner of JOHN ST. & BELLE VUE ST. FILEY.

The York City and County Bank, on the corner of Murray Street and West Street. Next to the bank is W.H. Hardwick's Federated footwear shop, which offered shoes in a 'genuine sale'. To the left is Scotter's, one of a number of general grocers in the town at the time.

Cliff House on the corner of Murray Street and John Street. Charlotte Brontë stayed here on several occasions in the 1850s. It is now a gift shop and café.

The First World War memorial in Murray Street, built on the open space given by George Nesfield Barrett to the Filey UDC in 1919.

Jackson's china shop at No. 31 Belle Vue Street, one of a row of three similar single-storey buildings next to the Belle Vue private hotel. It is now Cainscross & Sons, gentlemen's outfitters and militaria seller.

Above: The Convent of the Sacred Heart, at the top of Cargate Hill and on the corner of John Street, in 1905. In its early years a high school for girls was established here by the Sisters of Charity. It was closed in 1969. It was taken over by the district council and now houses a concert hall, the Evron Centre and visitor information office.

Left: Heptinstall's was a bakery and confectionery shop in John Street. The handcart parked outside was used for making deliveries around the town and advertised their catering business.

Right: This shop at No. 10 John Street was gutted by a fire on 8 January 1920 which also caused damage to the premises on the right in the picture. It would be interesting to know whether any of the chocolate was damaged in the adjoining Maynard's sweet shop. It is situated opposite the present-day community centre.

Below: Haxby's at No. 11 Rutland Street was a general furniture store. They produced much of their own stock and undertook joinery work.

Mrs R. Stockdale's shop in John Street. Rose, the proprietor, can just be seen in the doorway while her niece, Enid, is attending to the display of fruit and vegetables.

Built on a site in Brooklands, the opening of St Mary's church in 1904 was much welcomed by both the resident and visiting Roman Catholic community. In the same year the Sisters of Charity opened the Convent of the Sacred Heart in John Street.

Station Avenue extended inland from Murray Street. On the left, under the trees in this 1924 view, is the London City Bank. The spire is that of the Trinity Methodist church which had just been reopened after a fire.

An artist's impression of the Trinity Methodist church at the height of the blaze in December 1918 which destroyed much of the fabric. The cause of the fire was never determined. A rebuilding programme was immediately put into effect and the church reopened on 7 March 1923.

Station Avenue led to the LNER station which was opened in 1847. Its opening allowed improved access for the developing tourist trade, and gave the town's fishing industry quicker access to potential markets. This view shows the engine shed which stood on the far side of the level crossing. This is now the site of the Silver Birches care home.

A photograph by W. Fisher of St John's church in West Street at the junction with Rutland Street. Built in the Gothic style it provided a more convenient place of worship for the Anglican community in the expanding southern end of the town.

West Avenue, formerly West Street, is a relatively recent extension with its residential terraces and large individual houses. It leads along to Glen Gardens and Filey Golf Club.

Clarence House was built in Victorian times as a high-class private boarding and day school for girls, run by a Miss McCallim. In the 1930s it became a hotel before briefly becoming a youth hostel. It is now divided into private apartments.

These terraced houses in Southdene provided guest house accommodation for summer visitors. The building at the top of the terrace was the Royal Crescent Hotel and the Hotel Vaults.

four

The Promenade

FILEY, BEACH PROMENADE

The nineteenth/twentieth century development of private housing and small hotels along the seafront was random, haphazard and at the mercy of the waves until the sea wall was constructed. The stone-built house was once the home of John Unett, son of the planner of the New Filey Crescent and Gardens. It is now the Downcliff Hotel.

An earlier image of the Promenade, captured by W. Fisher of Filey as part of a series of stereoscopic photographs. The recently completed Spa Saloon, seen here on the left, was used for a variety of cultural entertainments. The road surface leaves something to be desired.

The Spa, with its continental design, became an assembly hall and lodging house known as Ackworth House. It later became one of the Christian Holidays Association's guest houses.

A group of Wesleyan scholars gathered together on the veranda of Ackworth House, c. 1885. During the late nineteenth century there was a strong movement towards Methodism in the town, particularly amongst the fishing community. This early picture was taken prior to the addition of the portico and iron balustrade at the front of the building.

Filey from Sands. Valentine's Series.

A general view of the Promenade showing Unett's rubble-and-concrete sea wall. The building of the new sea wall started in 1892 and ran along the front of the foreshore.

The new sea wall was completed by the contractor James Dickson of St Albans in 1894. The wall, built as a reflecting arch with a coping above to throw back the waves, averaged 7 metres in height. Work began at the Church Ravine slipway and continued southwards to the Crescent Hill slipway – some 700 metres. Much of the stone used was brought from the Brigg by light rail.

At this point on the Promenade, at the foot of Cargate Hill, a slipway was made through the sea wall to allow boats access to the beach. This was spanned by an elaborate cast-iron bridge.

The protection afforded by the new sea wall to buildings at the southern end of the Promenade is illustrated by a storm in the summer of 1906, shown here in this Fisher series postcard. Note the height of the breaking waves in relation to the wary onlookers and the debris littering the road.

Edwardian Filey. The carriages stand waiting while their passengers enjoy a bracing walk along the south end of the Promenade.

Northcliffe is a significant private house with magnificent views of the bay. It was built at the top of Cargate Hill for a member of the Clark family, the successful cotton manufacturers.

Midway along the Promenade is Cargate Hill. The horse-drawn traffic brought visitors down to the beach and then took them back up the hill into the town. Kingstone Cottage, half hidden in the trees, was demolished in order to extend Northcliffe Gardens.

The north end of the Promenade, viewed from the Coble Landing. The third building along featuring the flagpole is the coastguard station. Two maroons would be fired from the front lawn to summon the lifeboat crew in an emergency. The sender of this postcard, in 1930, said that she had recently seen the Graff Zeppelin airship pass over the bay.

A. Pashby's shellfish stall was one of those situated on the slipway at the foot of Cargate Hill, serving customers in the 1950s.

The foreshore at the foot of Sand Hill. The buildings along Cliff Top are those of Old Filey.

In this 1947 view there can be seen, on the left, the white hut where beach tents could be hired. The small kiosk in the centre sold fresh crabs and lobsters which could be dressed to order. The stalls to the right offered visitors teas, cigarettes and other refreshments.

By the 1950s there was greater investment along the promenade. The boating lake doubled as a toddlers' paddling pool. There was also a small fair, kiosks for refreshments, weather shelters and public conveniences.

Children's amusement park on the foreshore near the Coble Landing.

On a sunny day many visitors would take the air either along the Promenade or sands. Most would spend time gazing out to sea watching the yawls or the smaller fishing cobles.

five

Church Ravine
and
St Oswald's

FILEY. THE RAVINE

Above: This valley, immediately to the north of Filey, was most likely formed by the water running from the melting ice sheets covering the north of Britain during the Ice Age. Prior to the twentieth century the Ravine marked the boundary between the north and east Ridings.

Left: At one time the valley sides were almost devoid of trees until landscaping took place in the late 1870s. During this period the stream, Filey Beck, was also culverted.

Both donkey- and horse-drawn traffic would find the steady climb up the Ravine relatively easy.

The car, with lady driver and passenger, on its way down the Ravine. It has just passed beneath the metal bridge which enabled pedestrians to cross over the valley between Old Filey and St Oswald's church. It replaced a lower-level stone bridge which was damaged in a storm in the 1850s.

Left: Three water carriers filling up at one of the freshwater springs which issued out of the north side of the Ravine, below where the footbridge now stands. They would supply water to such boats as the Scottish herring fleet and others which landed in the bay for fresh provisions. The position of the spring is now recorded by a plaque.

Below: Even in the 1930s the Ravine was a convenient place for motorists to park their cars when spending a day on the beach.

The Ravine, Filey

Right: This winter view of the Ravine in January 1909 was the result of a very heavy hoar frost.

Below: It is somewhat strange that St Oswald's, Filey's relatively large parish church, should be built in such exposed isolation on the north side of the Ravine in the North Riding of Yorkshire, at some distance from its faithful congregation.

Filey Parish Church, (Interior)

Above: The church is late Norman in origin, *c.* 1180. This can be seen in the nave pillars, clerestory windows and main south door. Contrary to early intentions the squat tower was placed centrally and was surmounted by a fish-shaped weathervane which was symbolic of both Christianity and the local village trade.

Left: Many of Filey's clergy have enjoyed long incumbencies, not least the Revd Canon Arthur Neville Cooper, MA (1880-1935). He was known as the 'walking parson' and visited many European capitals and diocesan meetings travelling on foot, producing books about his journeys. He did much local charity work amongst distressed fishing families, and voiced his strong opinion on local issues.

six

Coble Landing
and Lifeboat

The Coble Landing has provided a safe haven for the fishing boats or 'cobles' of Filey men since times before the Domesday survey. This artistic image does something to capture and convey a nostalgic and endearing scene.

In its heyday, in the mid-1800s, the Filey coble fleet numbered over eighty-five boats. As many as 400 men – about half the population – were engaged in some way with the activity and support of the industry. Many of the cobles would be landed on the end of the Promenade and at the foot of the Church Ravine. Boat builders involved with construction and repairs included Cambridge's and Jenkinson's.

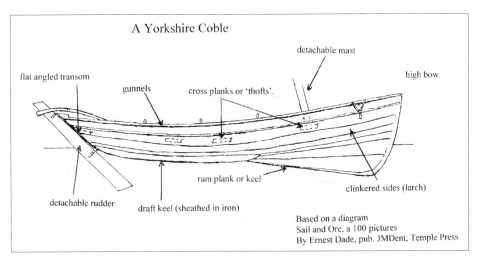

A Yorkshire Coble

detachable mast

flat angled transom

high bow

gunnels

cross planks or 'thofts'.

ram plank or keel

clinkered sides (larch)

detachable rudder

draft keel (sheathed in iron)

Based on a diagram
Sail and Ore, a 100 pictures
By Ernest Dade, pub. JMDent, Temple Press

Every fishing village along the Yorkshire coast would have had their own variations in the design of these open-sea boats, in order to suit local conditions and different methods of launching. The designs may well date back to the Viking longships centuries ago. Generally, the boats would have a high, solid bow and narrow, steeply sloping transom stern that would support a detachable rudder extending beneath the coble by 1.5 metres or so. From the central 'ram' plank, or keel, the larch, clinkered-planked sides would be raised up and fixed over 'grown' oak ribs, up to the gunnels. Crossway planks or 'thofts' would carry the steeply angled mast and provide seats for rowing and steering. These boats were of a very shallow draft and light in weight, and were protected underneath, when grounding, by oak, 'draft' keels sheathed with iron chaffing strips. The Filey fishermen of the 1900s tended to favour slightly smaller cobles of about 8.25 metres in length, which had a beam of about 2.25 metres.

Fishing was done during the very early hours of the morning, usually by a crew of three, using either a long line of baited hooks or a shallow drift net. The catch would be landed soon after first light to catch the Yorkshire and Midland markets. Smaller cobles, with a crew of two, would retrieve crabs and lobsters from 'pots' laid out around the Brigg and would fish for salmon when it was in season.

Cobles would be landed stern first and lifted, by a team of other fisherman with the aid of the swell, on to cranked, wooden-axled beams supported by sturdy wooden cartwheels. Teams of up to three horses, working in tandem, would enter the surf, turn without command and after being hitched would tow the coble up the slipway.

The cobles were usually painted in strong contrasting colours – often red, blue and white. Their names might reflect such virtues as trust, confidence, faith and hope; for example, Unity, Diligence, Good Intent and Charity.

After the Second World War tractors replaced horses, cranked steel axles replaced wooden beams and car wheels replaced cartwheels – all of which made it easier to bring cobles ashore, as shown in this artistic image.

The Filey cobles were usually registered at Scarborough with a number prefixed S.H., being the first and last letters of Scarborough. In recent years the fleet has dwindled to barely half a dozen cobles and the evocative smell of fish has almost disappeared.

Left: Two fishermen enjoying a moment of relaxation, *c.* 1890. The gentleman on the left is wearing a traditional 'gansey'. Each family would invariably have their own recognisable design which was a personal combination of cable, zig-zag, ladder, double moss or diamond stitch. The arms were almost always knitted in a Betty Martin stitch and the whole garment would take about fifty hours to make.

Below: This Edwardian scene shows one of the many Filey yawls which were beached for unloading. Over thirty such vessels, crewed by Filey men, were based at Scarborough, which was a deep water port. With a crew of seven they would fish for several days well out into the North Sea, returning to land their catch. Other commodities such as coal and grain might also be brought in.

Over the last 150 years facilities for visitors to the Coble Landing have gradually grown, with the introduction of amusement arcades, cafés, fast-food outlets, shops, chalets, pony rides and so on.

'BONZO' FILEY'S FAMOUS PET SEAL

One of the attractions on show at the Coble Landing in the 1930s was Bonzo the seal, exhibited by his keeper Jack 'Bonso' Jenkinson, who also kept the family's shellfish stall. The creature was found abandoned on the Brigg as a pup and was rescued by Jack's uncle.

Filey, with its convenient slipway, firm sands and sheltered bay was ideal for yachtsmen. Many travelled long distances to take part in the annual Filey Bay Regatta each July, as well as other offshore races throughout the year.

In 1823 the people of Filey established their own independent lifeboat with locally raised funds. This was based on the foreshore at the foot of Cargate Hill. The RNLI adopted the service in 1852. The *Hallon* was the third lifeboat of that name sponsored by R.W. Hallon, the Lord Mayor of York.

To launch the lifeboat it had to be towed down on to the beach and into the surf by a team of six trained horses. These were kept in readiness in a cliff-top field by Geoffrey Colling of Queen Street. The steel carriage would then be swung round, angled down and the boat would run on rollers into the water.

The arrival of a new lifeboat was something of an occasion. On 4 May 1907 a naming and blessing ceremony for *Hallon III* was held on the beach in front of a large crowd and other invited dignitaries. It is interesting to see members of the choir wearing their cloth caps.

In 1889 the RNLI built a new station on the Coble Landing to house the *Hallon* lifeboats. They were all self-righting boats propelled by oar and sail until the arrival of the *Cuttle*, which was powered by petrol engine. Here, in 1907, John Crimlisk (left) and Frankie Baxter proudly represented the many local and skilled fishermen who were eager to serve the Institution.

George 'Dingle' Scales was a much respected and experienced lifeboat cox who served between 1889 and 1907. He can be seen wearing a cork lifeboat jacket, which was the standard issue by the RNLI at the time. He supervised many rescue operations during his time.

Filey held an annual lifeboat day when the boats were ceremoniously pulled through the town to raise funds for the RNLI and then launched from the Coble Landing. This view of proceedings in 1934 shows *Hallon III* being pulled by the newly arrived RNLI tractor equipped with wheel tracks.

The Yorkshire coast is the site of many shipwrecks and Filey Bay was no exception. Here, a small group of onlookers have gathered to see the *Truro*, a steam drifter which ran aground in June 1907 on the rocks below the chalk cliffs on the south of Filey Bay. It was presumably re-floated as it has not been listed as a wreck.

In April 1915 the SS *Eglantine*, a 1,300-ton collier bound from Tyneside to Le Havre, collided with the Brigg while trying to avoid the attentions of a German submarine. The crew were rescued by the *Hallon III* lifeboat but their vessel was a total loss.

The *Lyng*, a 648-ton Norwegian herring fleet support ship, ran onto the Brigg in fog on 30 January 1928 and broke up soon after. It is now a popular target for the local diving club.

seven

The Sands

Above: During Victorian times visits to the beach became increasingly fashionable, though they were at first a very formal occasion. Suitably equipped with shelter tent, seating, hampers and more, this family is settling down for a picnic.

Left: Nannies, governesses and nursery maids, employed by the more wealthy visitors to Filey, would have found the sands a popular place to take the children in their care for a breath of fresh air and sunshine.

Opposite below: A family enjoying the usual pleasure and activities on the sands in less formal times. Feel free to admire their sandcastle.

Here a group of Edwardians are enjoying an impromptu game of beach cricket, *c.* 1904. Filey Bay is blessed with over six miles of firm, tide-washed sands which stretch from the Brigg in the north to Speeton Cliffs in the south.

FILEY MOTOR RACES JUNE 1905.
M' CECIL EDGE ON HIS 90 HP NAPIER, AFTER BREAKING THE YORKSHIRE MILE RECORD

The winner of the time trials was Mr Cecil Edge from London in his 90hp Napier which achieved a speed of 71.5mph. Prizes were awarded at a special dinner held at the Royal Crescent Hotel, which was the headquarters for the occasion.

Opposite above: The sands were considered a suitable venue for the Yorkshire Automobile Club's inaugural speed trials. This was held on the Whitsuntide Monday of 1905 along a two-mile course which was marked with a ploughed furrow. There were eight classes for the various entrants and a crowd of over 2,000 was reported to have witnessed the spectacle.

Right: A Blackburn Mercury monoplane flying over Filey Beach, *c.* 1911. The large expanse of sand was ideal for the training of pilots at Filey Flying School near Primrose Valley. The Blackburn Aircraft Company also built a slipway, hanger and staff accommodation to facilitate the testing of their machines.

Below: The reverse of this card is autographed by R. Blackburn, OBE, AMICE, FRAES, MIME, who designed the aircraft in his own workshops in Leeds. They were brought by rail to Filey where they were assembled and flown.

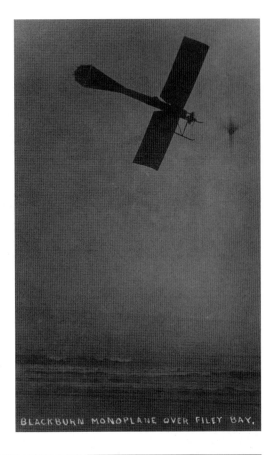

BLACKBURN MONOPLANE OVER FILEY BAY.

POST CARD. £15

STAMP

✳

HERE

This space for communication   The address to be written here

W. Fisher, 34 Belle Vue St., Filey

RBlackburn

The wings of the Mercury were supported by guy wires attached to a central pylon in front of the cockpit. Steering was achieved by means of a wheel connected by cables to the tail fin. The landing gear consisted of four sturdy cycle wheels on either side of two skids. The plane was most likely to have been flown by self-taught Bentfield C. Hucks, who is standing third from the left.

In the early 1900s, those wishing to take a dip in the sea might hire one of the large-wheeled bathing machines from Mr H. Wright. These were gradually replaced by the smaller-wheeled beach huts. Here they have been pulled up onto the Crescent Hill slipway to be clear of the incoming tide.

Above: The bathing machines were pulled down to the water's edge and the bathers would enter the sea down some steps. Beach huts would be similarly pulled into position on the sands by horses.

Right: Kitty Hodgson was one of the bathing attendants who would carry water down to the bathing huts for the bathers to wash the salty water from their bodies.

Beach tents became increasingly popular shortly before the Second World War. These could be hired by the public, for the day or week, from Burr & Fell Tent Proprietors. The pale-green canvas tent shelters were set up over an expanding metal and wood frame, which was mounted on a skidded pallet board. When not in use they would be stored on racks on the cliff side.

The tents would be arranged in semicircles along the beach, each labelled with the hirer's name. If a high tide approached, gangs of students would drag them up to the foot of the cliffs.

The Pierrots. Filey.

Most visitors to the beach wanted some form of entertainment. At the close of the nineteenth century, Ernest Taylor, himself a former Catlin's Pierrot from Bridlington, established his own troupe called the Royal Filey Pierrots in 1895. At first they would normally perform their routine of vocals, music, comedy and instrumentals on the sands at the foot of Martin's Barrier. A bottle would be taken round in the hope of collecting sufficient funds to pay for a night's lodgings. Note the beach photographer's kiosk, with camera and tripod at the ready.

Ernest Taylor (seated), who adopted the stage name Andie Caine, was a skilled and respected singer and banjo player. Like several others in the troupe he became a resident of Filey, successfully entertaining visitors for over forty-five years until his death in 1941. During the winter months he would often appear in one of the London pantomimes.

Donkey, pony and cart rides have always been a popular seaside attraction and rides could be obtained at various points along the beach, such as here at the foot of Crescent Hill. At the end of a long day the pony carts would often take visitors back up into the town.

Filey Sands was also a popular place for the many riding clubs in the district. In winter the race horses would often be brought down to the beach for exercising when the inland gallops were frozen.

Part of the beach below Martin's Barrier was designated a children's corner. Here it was possible to enjoy an ice cream, enter sandcastle-building competitions, have one's photograph taken, enter a race or two on sports day, enjoy a Punch and Judy show, hire a rubber dinghy, and much more.

The coconut shy was also a regular feature on the Sands for many years in the children's corner.

Martin's Barrier was built in 1889 by Edwin Martin, a Huddersfield mill owner, to protect his newly acquired Ravine villa estate (now the Glen Gardens) from rapid coastal erosion. To it were added various shelters and a café. It survived admirably until it was seriously damaged in a storm in January 1953. It was replaced by the Royal Parade in 1955.

Beachcombing was a popular pastime following a storm or particularly high tide. Items both natural and man-made, such as this First World War mine, could be found along the shoreline.

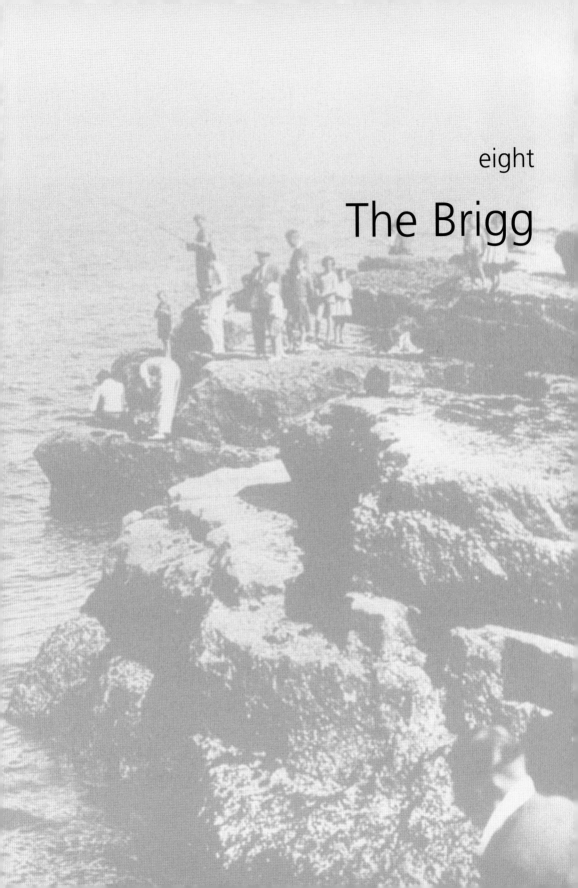

eight

The Brigg

The Brigg (to the right) is a 150-million-year-old reef of Jurassic oolitic rocks which projects out from beneath the cliffs of Carr Naze, which were formed from a thick deposit of glacial till laid down in successive Ice Ages over 15,000 years ago. The Brigg was designated a site of special scientific interest in 1985.

An intricate series of paths along both the top and foot of the cliffs have been created by the many centuries of visitors to the area. The remains of a Roman signal station have also been discovered on the top of the cliffs. On the northern edge, spa waters were located but these never became commercially viable.

This natural breakwater has been a great asset to Filey. Running several hundreds of metres out to sea before submerging below the waves, it has offered some protection to boats in the bay. At low tide it provides healthy and invigorating walks, but on stormy days waves breaking over the rocks can reach spectacular heights.

In the early 1900s visitors to the Brigg would often enjoy welcome refreshments which could be obtained from Nansen's Café. As one might expect, the building, being in such a vulnerable position, was often damaged in severe storms.

The Brigg has been a convenient source of building material for the construction of Filey's sea defence walls, as well as for some of the town's buildings. Much of the Brigg is now held in place by huge anchor bolts. The boulders to the right are now thought by marine archaeologists to be part of an artificial pier known as The Spittals, which is possibly Roman in origin.

The Brigg Café of the 1930s replaced an earlier refreshment building. It was itself wrecked by an exploding wartime mine which was washed up onto the Brigg in the autumn of 1939.

Fishing for codling with rod and line from the rocks was a popular pastime. Visitors could also join one of the many fishing parties which were brought out in the cobles to catch mackerel off the Brigg.

On a calm, warm day many visitors to Filey would enjoy a short trip round the bay on one of the cobles which operated at different points along the beach. This was known locally as 'spawing' and provided additional income for the boat owners. Passengers would be transferred between shore and boat on these specially designed handcarts.

Visitors to the Brigg could also be brought across the bay on one of the cobles. They would be assisted from the back of the coble on to the rocks by means of a walkway formed by the boat's rudder, here being held by George William Hunter.

Above: Those who ventured further round to the north side of the Brigg and Carr Naze would see the caves, known locally as 'doddles'. The first cave, with its 'Emperor's Pool' which is topped up at each high tide, is perhaps the largest.

Opposite: For a small tip guides such as Bobby Nolson, pictured here, would be on hand during busy times to assist visitors and to escort them round the Brigg, explaining some of the more interesting features. He would also be able to identify specimens retrieved from the rock pools.

FILEY BRIGG & CAVES, FILEY.   14.

Visitors to the north side were advised to leave well before high tide to avoid being trapped. This memorial tablet was cemented up on the rocks for many years at the point where Charles Paget, MP for Nottingham, and his wife Ellen were washed off and drowned by a freak wave in October 1873.

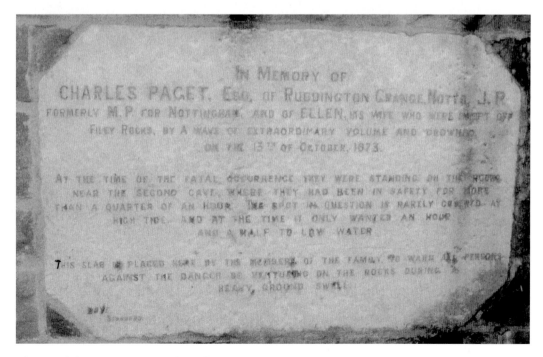

The 'Paget' plaque is now preserved in Filey Museum.

The distant rock upon which the visitors are standing, and which is the last to be submerged by a high rising tide, is known as High Brigg.

This new Brigg Café of the 1950s replaced the previous hut destroyed during the Second World War. Besides the usual beverages and confectionery, camera film was available and chairs could be hired.

Since 1850 a 'bell bouy' has been anchored several hundred metres off the end of the Brigg. It was set up by the elder brethren of Trinity House to warn ships of the position and dangers of the submerged reef of rocks. Besides being equipped with a flashing light and bell, its monotonous low moaning sound could be clearly heard as it rose and fell with each wave. It is still there and periodically it is lifted out of the water for servicing by a Trinity House vessel.

nine

Walter Fisher
and Filey Folk

Walter Fisher's horse-drawn cart, loaded with all the paraphernalia required by a professional photographer of the time, was a familiar sight around the district. He can be seen standing on the right in the bowler hat. Many of the images which recorded the passing of daily life in Filey were largely due to his perceptive and artistic photography. It is believed that he came to Filey for the first time from Norwich in 1857. He worked the summer season along the beach, the Promenade, the Coble Landing and the Crescent, taking photographs of the various visitors and selling them prints as a memento of their holiday. The art of photography was in its formative years at this time but Fisher quickly realised the potential that Filey had to offer and took up residence in the town. Over the years he captured on film a unique, evocative and valuable record of the changing scenes of Filey: its streets, landscapes, topical news items and everyday events; its local families, individual characters, and their trades and pastimes. Much of his work has been saved for all to enjoy through the efforts of his grandson, Fred Fisher, and John Crimlisk. The collection is now housed at the district council's archives and there is a permanent display at the museum in Queen Street. There is also an exhibition in the town's library.

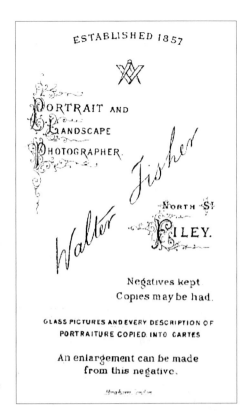

ESTABLISHED 1857

PORTRAIT AND
LANDSCAPE
PHOTOGRAPHER.

Walter Fisher

NORTH S!
FILEY.

Negatives kept
Copies may be had.

GLASS PICTURES AND EVERY DESCRIPTION OF
PORTRAITURE COPIED INTO CARTES

An enlargement can be made
from this negative.

Walter Fisher advertised, on the reverse of many of his portrait cards, his studio in North Street, which he established in 1857.

A portrait greetings card produced at Fisher's Belle Vue Street studio, sent to Dorothy from Robert Stephenson.

95

Left: An advertisement for Fisher's establishment in Belle Vue Street, which appeared in an early Filey town guide.

Below: Fisher's single-storey studio at No. 34 Belle Vue Street, which was located between John Street and the Belle Vue private hotel, *c.* 1885.

Fisher's house, shop and studio in Rutland Street.

Inside Fisher's Rutland Street studio, showing the choice of props and backdrops which might have been used in his portrait work.

An ox roast held in celebration of the coronation of King George V in 1911. It was held in an open space in Murray Street where the present post office now stands.

The Archbishop of York, Cosmo Gordon Lang, attended by Canon Cooper, at what is believed to be the opening of the Church of England infant school extension in Union Street, *c.* 1910.

Filey United Football Team, winners of the Filey Challenge Bowl 1896/97. In 1893 the team was an amalgamation of the Filey Town tradesmen's team, formed in 1889, and the Filey Red Stars, established in 1891 – the latter a team comprised largely of local fishermen, many of whom tragically lost their lives in a horrific storm.

Mr and Mrs Farrer's golden wedding, which was celebrated in May 1915. With the exception of Mrs Farrer, who was deaf and dumb, all those seated were blind, deaf and dumb. Canon Cooper is standing in the back row.

The 1st Huntingdonshire Cyclists Battalion undergoing training on a site in West Street, 1915. They were later sent off to France to serve in the First World War as first-aiders and messengers.

Girls, probably of the Church of England school in Scarborough Road, *c.* 1910. Elsie, the sender of the card, writes that 'they are not such a bad group'.

W. Mowthorpe, general blacksmith's. The premises later became Crimlisk & Lynn, builders and joiners. It was demolished in 1982 and is now the site of Boden's Plumbers, next to the Salvation Hall.

This trio of fishermen carrying their fishing lines ashore was captured by Fisher, *c.* 1900. From left to right they are William 'Cobby' Hunter, Matthew Colling and Frank Wheeler.

A 'flither' girl, possibly Susie Sayers. Such girls would scour the rocks up and down the coast for many miles, searching for limpets and other shell-fish. These would then be used to bait up the hooks on the fishing lines.

A water carrier, *c.* 1890. Barrels of fresh water would be carried down to the boats to replenish the drinking supplies.

Right: This card, posted in 1904 to a Mrs Knight of Reynolds Yard, Old Filey, shows a Filey fisherman proudly displaying a tabletop full of his collection of fishing-related items.

Below: The Filey Fishermens' Choir when they performed at the Methodist chapel, Halifax, in 1926. From left to right, front row: Edward Scales Jenkinson Jnr, Frank Hanson, E. Jenkinson. Middle row: Tom Willis, William 'Billie Calam' Cammish, Edward Scales Jenkinson Snr, Tom Crimlisk Snr, Tom Crimlisk Jnr. Back row: Matt Haxby Snr, Jimmy Douglas, Richard Wikkis, and Tom 'Tich' Jenkinson.

This team of egg-gatherers would work the cliffs at nearby Bempton at the height of the seabird breeding season in the late spring. Men wearing a harness and a large-pocketed waistcoat would be lowered several hundred metres down the vertical cliffs to collect the eggs, which would then be sold.

This well-loaded charabanc, registered in Bradford in 1906, is transporting a group of tourists to Filey, probably from Scarborough. This is the 12.30 p.m. run and the fare was 2s return. Protection from any possible rain looks scant.

ten

Butlin's

An aerial view of Butlin's holiday camp in its heyday in the 1960s, situated about one mile to the south of Filey. Many Filonians were apprehensive when Billy Butlin was given permission, in 1939, to develop this third site in Filey Bay (which became his pride and joy), following the success of his first camp at Skegness. When the Second World War broke out the War Ministry commandeered the site, but arranged with Butlin to finish the building so that it could serve as an RAF initial training wing, known as RAF Hunmanby Moor.

Accommodation for the 10,000 visitors was mainly in chalets which were small and basic, but cheerful and clean. Nearly 2,000 were built. Some visitors arrived at the camp in the morning to find their chalet waiting to be built, but by late afternoon it had been erected, decorated, furnished and equipped.

There were three main dining rooms – Kent, York and Windsor – each of which could serve over 2,000 meals in two sittings. Food was basic but wholesome, and lunch might consist of tomato soup, roast beef, roast and boiled potatoes, spring cabbage, steamed fruit pudding and custard.

Butlin's always provided a full and varied programme of first-class entertainment, which attracted both resident campers and the general public from a long way off. During the war, the Gaiety Theatre served as a storage depot. In the late 1950s it was renamed the Princes Theatre. Many redcoats developed their talents on this stage prior to becoming nationally famous.

BUTLIN'S FILEY
The Camp Train (Puffing Billy)

All aboard the camp train 'Puffing Billy', somewhat overstaffed with redcoats, so-called because of their distinctive dress. It was their duty to see that campers had a happy time and to help and entertain them during their stay.

FRENCH BAR, BUTLIN'S CAMP FILEY
PHOTO BY BUTLINS PHOTOGRAPHIC SERVICES LTD

Formerly the Kent Dining Room, it became the French Bar in 1956. At the time it boasted the longest bar in Great Britain at nearly 200 feet, with twenty ale pumps and sixty plus staff.

Dancing was a very popular leisure activity and many very good bands provided suitable music in the Viennese Ballroom during the season. Filey also hosted some very prestigious ballroom dance championships both for adults and juniors. It later became the Welcome Inn between 1955 and 1964.

The ballroom was later rebuilt as the Beachcomber's Bar in 1964. The décor had a Hawaiian theme and included a waterfall, lagoon and a river which was crossed by a bridge. A background film would be projected at various intervals to show moving clouds and an erupting volcano. Cocktails and bar meals would be served.

The boating lake was formed over what had been the wartime parade ground. Behind was the open-air swimming pool with its two fountains. Further behind that was the indoor pool, the stadium and the sports field. The Empire Theatre can be seen on the left.

The outdoor pool, with its deeper central area which was reserved for diving. The fountains at either end were part of the pool's filtration and purification system. They were illuminated at night.

The rowing boats were always very popular. Around the lake and through parts of the camp ran the Santa Fe railway track, here carrying the Butlin's Express.

A less energetic way to enjoy a trip on the water was to board the *Butlin Queen of the Lake*, a scaled-down replica of a Mississippi paddle steamer.

The indoor pools were opened in the mid-1950s. They were of varying depths to suit bathers of different ages and abilities. The female changing cubicles were at the far end and the Promenade Lounge, which overlooked the outdoor pool, was along the left-hand side. There were also underwater viewing windows around the sides of the main pool.

Billy Butlin had originally been a travelling showman touring the country with the fairs. He introduced dodgem cars into Britain. The Butlin's funfair offered the latest and most up-to-date rides which were all free to campers.

The Butlin's Filey amusement park similarly provided swings, a helter-skelter, a big wheel, side shows, a roller-coaster, and more.

Charlie, at over seven tons in weight and 10 feet in height, was the largest elephant in captivity. He was rescued from a failed zoo by Butlin and taken to his holiday camp in Ayr. With great publicity he was transferred to Filey by low loader. Following the death of his devoted mahout (keeper) Shikh Ibrahim, in 1961, Charlie became difficult and had to be put down. He was buried at the side of his elephant house.

BUTLIN'S FILEY
THE CHAIR LIFT

The Chairlift, opened in the early 1960s, ran over the top of Yellow Camp to the north-west of the site. Built by Mitchell Ropeways, it ran over a series of 45 feet high pylons between the main road and the beach. The Yellow Camp was built to house teenage visitors but was later used by those just requiring bed and breakfast.

Above: Campers were only a few minutes walk away from Filey Beach near Hunmanby Gap.

Opposite: Butlin was keen to promote the reopening of his Filey Camp when the Second World War had ended. Dare Devil Peggy's 'Death Dive by Daylight', in 1946, where she jumped from the top of a 75 feet high tower into a water tank enveloped in flames, attracted a large crowd.

CAMP CHURCH (C•FE) BUTLINS HOLIDAY CAMP FILEY

The camp had both a Catholic church and a Church of England, which, when first built, was known as the church of St Alban's. Services were held every day.

Butlin's, at its height, had its own 'run-round' rail terminus off the main Scarborough to Bridlington line. Visitors from the Midlands were brought to and from the camp on Saturdays. The terminus would also be used by those on day excursions to the camp. Pictured here is a Class K1 No. 62005 engine. This Saturday-only service, opened in May 1947, was finally withdrawn in 1977.

In the camp a children's nursery or creche was provided to enable parents to enjoy a few moments of peace. In the evenings a listening service was available along the chalet lines which enabled parents to be called up in the event of a problem.

Butlin's employed a large team of gardeners to tend and keep the flower borders in tip-top condition for the visitors to enjoy on this 800-acre site. Here, the donkeys are being exercised on the lawn in front of the Kent Dining Hall.

Another area of the camp set aside for younger visitors to explore had haunted castles and crooked houses. There was also a helter-skelter and the usual variety of playground equipment.

Originally known as the North Theatre it was renamed the Empire in the early 1950s. During the war years it was the station's cinema and continued as such until closure of the camp in 1983.

eleven

Round and About

Muston Mill on the Muston Road. The sails and head gear, which were in a poor condition, were finally destroyed during a gale in 1920. It is just possible to read the name Barmby of Muston on the side of the cart. He was the miller at the time.

Muston, on the outskirts of Filey, is a typical small farming village, with a main street of cottages, Muston Hall, the Ship Inn and All Saints church. This 1907 postcard shows pupils outside the school, which was also an essential part of this village community.

Filey Golf Club was established in 1897 to the north of the town, but moved to its present site at the southern end of West Avenue two years later. The original 'New Links' course, designed by James Braid, with its lush fairways and excellent views to all parts of Filey Bay, has always been a popular attraction. It now has an additional nine-hole academy course and new clubhouse.

In 1951, just to the north of the Coble Landing, Filey Sailing Club built a slipway and clubhouse at the foot of the Pampletine Cliffs. Due to severe landslides in 1994 the clubhouse has been rebuilt with additional facilities. The club is now approached from the clifftop at Country Park.

The Primrose Valley lies a mile to the south of Filey and is another of the many small ravines that run down to the sea. Alongside runs a track which enables pedestrians to gain access to the sands.

In summer, the motorised Primrose Puffer Train transports passengers between the beach and the top of the valley.

Many children over the years have developed their civil engineering skills by altering the watercourse that trickles down the Primrose Valley and across the beach.

The 'Long Whine' at the head of Primrose Valley was once a small quiet settlement with a few small hotels such as The Linkfield, as well as attractive houses, holiday cottages, wooden bungalows and private schools.

Southcliff, in Primrose Valley, was at one time a boys' boarding and day school which had been transferred from South Crescent in Filey. In more recent times it became a hotel but it is now a tavern, fast-food outlet, and shopping and entertainment centre. It now serves the needs of holidaymakers staying at the many caravan sites which have grown up nearby over the years.

Habershon House is a children's convalescent home belonging to the Rotherham Education Authority. It is also used as a youth field-study centre.

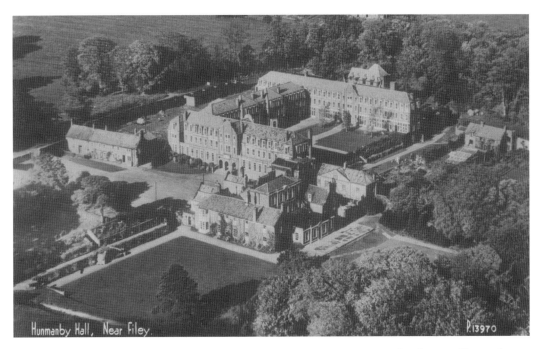

Hunmanby Hall, Near Filey.　P.13970

Inland from Primrose Valley lies Hunmanby, at one time an important agricultural centre. Hunmanby Hall was another building constructed extensively with stone obtained from Filey Brigg. It was the ancestoral seat of the Osbaldestone's, a renowned hunting family. In 1928 it became a girls' boarding school.

Hunmanby Gap was another quiet access point to the beach. It later became overwhelmed when the Butlin's holiday camp developed nearby in the 1950s.

Some four miles south of Filey lies Reighton with its ancient Norman church and reputation for being the haunt of smugglers. The sands have always been popular with picnickers and a holiday village has recently developed here.

BEACH AND SPEETON CLIFFS, PRIMROSE VALLEY NEAR FILEY   L 2854

Speeton Beach is the last place round the bay where the sands are accessible. Southwards the glacial cliffs give way to the chalky ramparts of Bempton and Flamborough.

Flamborough North Landing provides a safe but steep refuge for a few fishing boats and the remaining Flamborough Lifeboat House. Cobles can take visitors out from the beach to view the many fascinating sea caves, 'doors' and stacks carved into the chalk by the erosion of the waves.

The lighthouse, built in 1806 by local builder John Matson, stands 85 feet high, and its light is 220 feet above sea level. The light flashes four times every fifteen seconds; its beam radiates to all parts of Filey Bay and out to sea for over twenty miles.

Other local titles published by Tempus

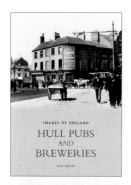

Hull Pubs and Breweries

PAUL GIBSON

As social centres and places of entertainment, Hull's old pubs hold an important place in the life of the city. *Hull Pubs and Breweries* uses over 200 photographs and other ephemera to take the reader on a journey through the rich architectural diversity available within the city's many historic and important pub buildings. This volume also features scenes from the breweries, with archive images of the vehicles, the staff and many long-lost pubs.

0 7524 3284 2

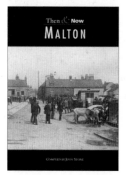

Malton Then & Now

COMPILED BY JOHN STONE

The ancient Yorkshire market town of Malton has seen many changes over the years and this enthralling book sets out to illustrate some of them using 'then and now' pairs of photographs, which illustrate dramatically how differently we live today. All who know Malton will enjoy this nostalgic look at the town, seen through the lenses of photographers separated by up to a century.

0 7524 2608 7

Scarborough Then & Now

COLIN WATERS

Scarborough has changed greatly from the days when staid Victorian ladies and gentlemen sought the benefits of the spa waters and a quick dip in the ocean. This fascinating collection of images takes the reader on a nostalgic trip back to a time when Scarborough served as a commercial port and shipbuilding centre and the herring fishing trade thrived. Transport, work and leisure pursuits are all explored in detail, and this book will provide much enjoyment for both residents and visitors alike.

0 7524 3618 X

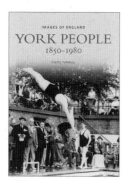

York People 1850-1980

YVETTE TURNBULL

This absorbing collection offers a glimpse into the lives of some of the people who shaped the history and character of this great city in the nineteenth and twentieth centuries. The emphasis throughout is on ordinary people actually living – at work and at home, at peace and at war, in worship and celebration: there is something here for everyone who has an interest in the city of York.

0 7524 3716 X

If you are interested in purchasing other books published by Tempus, or in case you have difficulty finding any Tempus books in your local bookshop, you can also place orders directly through our website

www.tempus-publishing.com